HAPPY SONG
Sing-Alongs

ABC Chicka Boom with Me

and Other
Phonemic Awareness/Phonics
Songs & Activities

Guitar and Musical Arrangements
David Plummer

Vocals
John Archambault and David Plummer

Children's Vocals
Arie Archambault and Tyler Plummer

Activities Written by
Kim Cernek
John Archambault

Illustrator:
Darcy Tom

Editor:
Kim Cernek

Project Director:
Carolea Williams

Table of Contents

Introduction 3

Chicka Chicka Boom Boom
Song Lyrics 5
Activities 6

B-A Bay
Song Lyrics 15
Activities 16

Braggin' Dragon
Song Lyrics 21
Activities 22

Chicka Chicka Funk
Song Lyrics 26
Activities 27

We Are Hippopotamus
Song Lyrics 31
Activities 32

The Happapatamus
Song Lyrics 36
Activities 37

Alphabet Zoo/The Name Game
Song Lyrics 40
Activities 42

Jump Rope Rhymes
Song Lyrics 47
Activities 48

Splish! Splash! Splash!
Song Lyrics 52
Activities 53

The Long and the Short of It
Song Lyrics 57
Activities 58

Student Award Reproducible 63

Literature Links 64

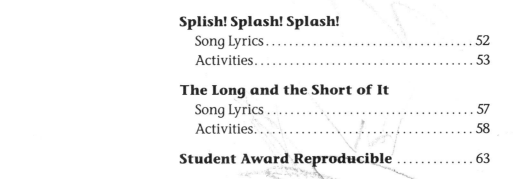

Introduction

With a whirl and a jiggle and a twirl and a giggle, music makes learning happen! Children respond to the way hippy, happy lyrics rouse something inside and snippy, snappy rhythms send all those things on the outside (like fingers and toes) into action. Music inspires a medley of movement, motivation, and minds in motion—all of which contribute to successful learning.

The *Happy Song Sing-Alongs* series pairs uplifting and playful music written and performed by renowned children's authors and musicians, John Archambault and David Plummer, with creative classroom activities. The goal of the *Happy Song Sing-Alongs* series is to promote the three Rs of learning—rhyme, rhythm, and retention—as the means for developing both academic skills and positive attitudes towards self, others, and nature.

Music enhances the physical, emotional, and intellectual well-being of a child. A young listener who is physically responding to a snappy rhythm has a relaxed mind that is open to greater creativity. A student who is absorbed in a moving melody is emotionally prepared to try new things without fear of failure. A child who is exposed to the patterns and rhythms inherent in music is better able to retain new knowledge.

Combine the benefits of music—heightened creativity, motivation, and retention—with fun activities that encourage students to explore the basic skills and concepts presented in the songs, and you have a phenomenal resource for preparing students to become successful learners.

Developing Phonemic Awareness/Phonics Skills

ABC Chicka Boom with Me combines the benefits of music and playful fun with phonemic-awareness and phonics skills. Phonemic-awareness development occurs in stages. Emergent readers must have extensive exposure to word patterns through rhythm and rhyme. Students must also be able to listen for sounds within a word before being able to sequence, separate, and manipulate these sounds. This ability precedes phonics instruction, which emphasizes the relationship between a sound and its written form (i.e., a letter). The activities in this book are designed to give students practice with these important beginning reading skills within the context of Archambault and Plummer's uplifting, literacy-oriented songs.

Various phonological skills are presented in the activities. Children will practice identifying similar word patterns (sound matching), listen for spoken syllables (syllable counting), identify onsets and rimes (syllable splitting), and blend individual sounds to form a word (phoneme blending). These activities will also have students identify where a given sound is heard in a word (approximation), count the number of phonemes in a word (phoneme counting), and identify individual sounds within a word (phoneme segmentation). Students will also distinguish between beginning, middle, and ending sounds in a word (phoneme isolation) before substituting (phoneme substitution) or omitting (phoneme deletion) them.

Phonics practice is introduced in many of the activities as students are invited to connect the sounds they hear in the songs with their written form. Children will also be given opportunities to become familiar with language patterns, strengthen vocabulary development, and improve diction in varied educational environments.

Components of *ABC Chicka Boom with Me*
This resource includes the following materials:
- Eleven warm, spirited **songs** that will captivate your students' imaginations while exposing them to the sounds and patterns of oral language.

- Reproducible **lyrics** of each song that can be transferred to overhead transparencies, poster board, chart paper, or sentence strips so that students can sing along.

- **Activities** that incorporate one or more of the following phonemic-awareness skills: sound matching; syllable counting and splitting; approximation; and phoneme blending, isolation, counting, segmentation, substitution, and deletion.

- **Cross-curricular connections** to areas that include writing, math, critical thinking, physical education, and art.

- Reproducible **activity patterns** that can also be used as room decorations and stationery.

- **Word families lists** that give you a handy resource for implementing activities that require words that follow specific patterns.

- **Alphabet cards** for use in activities that involve matching letters with their sounds.

- **Literature links** that correlate with the themes of the songs and support the goals of phonemic awareness.

- A **student award** reproducible to present to your students in celebration of their progress as readers.

Anticipate that your students will ask you to play *ABC Chicka Boom with Me* over and over again. The music is just too happy to resist singing along. Treat your students to the music and activities and you will see confident, successful readers develop as a result!

Chicka Chicka Boom Boom

A told B and B told C,
"I'll meet you at the top of the
   coconut tree."
"Whee," said D to E, F, G,
"I'll beat you to the top of the
   coconut tree."
Chicka chicka boom boom.
Will there be enough room?

Here comes H up the coconut tree.
And I and J and tag-along K—
All on their way up the coconut
   tree.
Chicka chicka boom boom.
Will there be enough room?

Look who's coming—it's L, M, N, O, P.
And Q, R, S and T, U, V.
Still more—W and X, Y, Z.
The whole alphabet's up the . . .
Oh! No!
Chicka chicka boom boom!

Skit, skat, skoodle-doot,
Flip, flop, flee.
Everybody running to the coconut
   tree.
Mamas and papas and uncles and
   aunts
Hug their little dears and dust
   their pants.
"Help us up," cried A, B, C.

Next from the pileup, skinned-
   knee D.
And stubbed-toe E and
   patched-up F.
Then comes G all out of breath.
H is tangled up with I.
J and K are about to cry.
L is knotted like a tie.
M is looped. N is stooped.
O is twisted—alley-oop.

Skit, skat, skoodle-doot,
Flip, flop, flee.
Look who's coming—
It's black-eyed P.
And Q, R, S and loose-tooth T.
And U, V, W—wiggle, jiggle free.
Last to come—X, Y, Z.
And the sun goes down on the
   coconut tree.

Chicka chicka boom boom.
Look there's a full moon.
A is out of bed and this is what
   he said,
"Dare, double dare, you can't
   catch me.
I'll beat you to the top of the
   coconut tree."

Chicka chicka boom boom.
Chicka chicka boom boom!

Chicka Chicka Chorus

The lyrics of "Chicka Chicka Boom Boom" are saturated with snappy sounds that students can't ignore. The following activities feature verses from the song that have been adapted for use in simple word games that promote phonemic awareness. Have students play these games during awkward transitional times or to keep them occupied in a lunchline or on a bus ride.

• This activity gives beginning readers practice isolating and matching sounds. Sing the following verse to the tune of "Chicka Chicka Boom Boom":

Chicka chicka boom boom,
Something in this room
***Starts** with the sound of the*
*/**b**/ in **bat**.*

Invite a student to point to an object in the room or name another word that begins with the same sound. Change the bolded parts of the chant and play again.

• This activity gives students practice identifying the sequence of sounds. Arrange students in a circle or line. Have students identify the phoneme described in the following verse:

Students: *Skit, skat, skoodle-doot,*
Flip, flop, flee.

Teacher: *I wonder what the **ending** sound of **cat** could be?*

Students: */**t**/*

Have the next student in line take over the part of the teacher and invite the class to repeat the chant. Encourage students to use other sounds at different positions (e.g., beginning, middle, or end) in spelling words or words from the Word Families List.

• Try this fun way for students to practice manipulating sounds through phoneme substitution. Have students sing the "Skit, skat, skoodle-doot" verse with different onsets, such as "Dit, dat, doodle-doot" or "Split, splat, sploodle-sploot." Record these new sounds on a cassette tape for students to enjoy in a listening center.

Coconutty Words

Materials
- ✓ Chicka Chicka Boom Boom by Bill Martin Jr. and John Archambault
- ✓ Alphabet Cards (pages 12–13)
- ✓ pocket chart

Read aloud *Chicka Chicka Boom Boom.* Explain to students that just as the letters of the alphabet were mixed up after their fall from the coconut tree, the letters in the following words have been scrambled. Select a word from the text of the book (e.g., *tree, room, way, hug, flip,* or *you*). Invite a student to pull the letters for that word from a set of Alphabet Cards and place the letters in random order in a pocket chart. For example, a student places the letters *e, r, t,* and *e* in the chart for *tree.* Invite the class to spell a word from the mixed-up letters. Suggest to students strategies for determining the word, such as looking for letter patterns and using the process of elimination.

Letter Hugs

Materials
- ✓ Hugging Friends reproducible (page 14)
- ✓ Alphabet Cards (pages 12–13)
- ✓ chart paper
- ✓ scissors
- ✓ tape

Some of the letters in "Chicka Chicka Boom Boom" needed a hug after they fell from the coconut tree. Explain to students that some letters of the alphabet "hug" each other to form one sound. For example, *c* and *h* combine to make the /ch/ sound in *chicka*. Write student-generated lists of words with various digraphs (e.g., *th, sh,* and *ch*) or different blends (e.g., *bl, gr,* and *st*) on chart paper. Display lists for student reference. Distribute a copy of the Hugging Friends reproducible and a set of Alphabet Cards to each student. Have students place the *c* and *h* cards in the boxes on the reproducible. Challenge students to arrange other Alphabet Cards in the remaining boxes on the page to form words that begin with /ch/ (e.g., *chair, chin,* and *chip*). Repeat the activity with other blends and digraphs. To help students explore blends and digraphs that appear at the end of a word, rearrange the Hugging Friends reproducible. Cut the paper apart on the broken line, place the hugging friends at the other end, and tape the pieces back together before copying the page for each student. Repeat the activity, only this time have students create words that end with different blends and digraphs.

Alphabet Accidents

Materials
✓ "Chicka Chicka Boom Boom" song (page 5)
✓ drawing paper
✓ crayons or markers

Assign each student a letter of the alphabet. Invite students to write their letter across one side of a piece of paper. Have students turn their paper over and draw the letter, personified, after its fall from the coconut tree. For example, a student might show the letter *D* with skinned knees. Have students refer to "Chicka Chicka Boom Boom" for other ideas. Challenge students to create silly alliterative names for their letter character, such as "Dan the Dusty D."

You Can't Catch Me

Materials
✓ Alphabet Cards (pages 12–13)

Have students play this version of "Duck, Duck, Goose" to practice alphabetizing skills. Invite students to sit in a circle. Place an Alphabet Card (in random order) before each student. (If there are less than 26 students, be sure to distribute consecutive letters beginning with *a*. If there are more than 26 students, rotate students in and out after each round of play.) Stand in the middle of the circle, and have the class chant the following verse to the tune of "Chicka Chicka Boom Boom":

Chicka chicka boom boom.
Look there's a full moon.
***C** is out of bed and this is what he said . . .*

The person with the letter *c* card stands, walks around the circle, and taps the head of the student who holds the next letter in the alphabet. This student, letter *d*, stands and both children run around the circle in opposite directions while the rest of the class chants

"Dare, double dare, you can't catch me.
***D** is the letter that comes after me."*
We wonder who the winner of this race will be.

The first student to return to the empty space in the circle wins. The winner stands in the middle of the circle and starts the next round by calling a new letter.

Word Families List—Short Vowels

-ack: back, jack, pack, rack, sack, tack, black, clack, crack, quack, shack, snack, track

-ad: bad, dad, had, lad, mad, pad, sad, glad

-ag: bag, gag, lag, nag, rag, sag, tag, wag, drag, flag, shag, snag

-am: dam, ham, jam, ram, cram, slam, wham

-an: ban, can, fan, man, pan, ran, tan, van, plan, scan

-ap: cap, gap, lap, map, nap, rap, sap, tap, clap, flap, slap, snap, trap

-at: at, bat, cat, fat, hat, mat, pat, rat, sat, vat, flat, that

-ed: bed, fed, led, red, wed, bred, fled, shed, sled, sped, shred

-ell: bell, cell, fell, sell, well, shell, smell, spell

-en: den, hen, men, pen, ten, then, when, wren

-est: best, jest, nest, rest, vest, west, chest, quest

-et: bet, get, jet, met, net, pet, set, vet, wet, yet, fret

-ick: kick, lick, pick, sick, tick, wick, brick, chick, quick, slick, thick, trick

-id: did, hid, kid, lid, rid, slid, squid

-ig: big, dig, fig, jig, pig, rig, wig, twig

ABC Chicka Boom with Me © 1999 Creative Teaching Press

Word Families List—Short Vowels

-ill: bill, dill, fill, gill, hill, mill, pill, sill, will, chill, drill, frill, grill, skill, spill, still, thrill

-in: fin, kin, pin, tin, win, chin, grin, skin, spin, thin, twin

-ink: link, mink, pink, rink, sink, wink, blink, drink, stink, think, shrink

-ip: dip, hip, nip, sip, tip, chip, drip, flip, grip, ship, skip, slip, trip, whip

-it: bit, fit, hit, kit, lit, pit, sit, wit, grit, knit, quit, skit, slit, split

-ock: dock, lock, rock, sock, clock, flock, knock, shock, smock, stock

-og: dog, fog, hog, jog, log, clog, frog, smog

-op: hop, mop, pop, top, chop, drop, shop, stop

-ot: cot, dot, hot, lot, not, pot, rot, tot, knot, plot, spot, trot

-ub: dub, cub, hub, rub, sub, tub, club, grub, stub, scrub, shrub

-uck: buck, duck, luck, puck, suck, tuck, chuck, cluck, stuck, truck, struck

-ug: bug, dug, hug, jug, mug, rug, tug, drug, plug, slug, snug

-um: bum, gum, hum, sum, drum, plum

-un: bun, fun, nun, pun, run, sun, spun

-ut: cut, jut, nut, rut, shut, strut

ABC Chicka Boom with Me © 1999 Creative Teaching Press

Word Families List—Long Vowels

-ail: bail, fail, hail, jail, mail, nail, pail, rail, sail, tail, wail, frail, quail, snail, trail

-ain: gain, main, pain, rain, brain, chain, drain, grain, stain, train

-ake: bake, cake, lake, make, rake, take, wake, brake, flake, shake, snake, stake

-ame: came, fame, game, lame, same, tame, blame, flame

-ank: bank, rank, sank, tank, blank, clank, crank, flank, plank, spank, thank

-ate: fate, gate, late, mate, plate, skate, state

-eat: beat, heat, meat, neat, seat, treat, wheat

-eep: beep, deep, jeep, keep, peep, weep, creep, sheep, sleep, steep, sweep

-eet: feet, meet, sheet, sleet, sweet, street

-ice: dice, lice, mice, nice, rice, price, slice, spice, twice

-ide: hide, ride, side, tide, wide, bride, glide, pride, slide

-ime: dime, lime, mime, time, crime, prime

-ive: dive, five, hive, live, drive

-oat: boat, coat, goat, bloat, float, gloat, throat

-old: bold, cold, gold, hold, mold, sold, told

-ole: hole, mole, pole, stole, whole

-one: bone, cone, tone, zone, phone, stone

-ose: hose, nose, rose, close, those

-y: by, my, cry, fly, fry, ply, sly, try, why

Chicka Chicka Boom Boom

Alphabet Cards

a	b	c	d
e	f	g	h
i	j	k	l
m	n	o	p
q	r	s	t

Alphabet Cards

u	v	w	x
y	z	a	d
e	g	i	l
m	n	o	p
r	s	t	u

ABC Chicka Boom with Me © 1999 Creative Teaching Press

Chicka Chicka Boom Boom

Hugging Friends

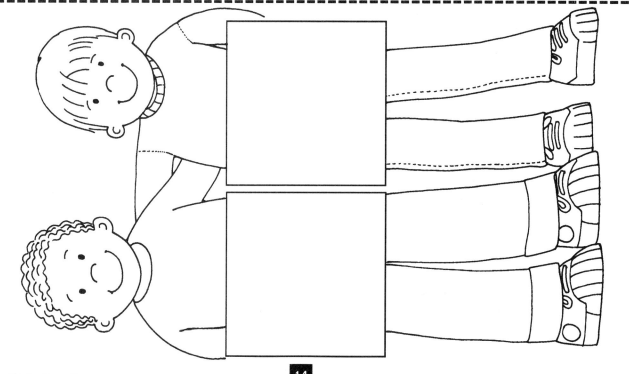

ABC Chicka Boom with Me © 1999 Creative Teaching Press

B-A Bay

B-a-bay
B-e-bee
B-i-biddee bye
B-o-bo
Biddee bye bo
B-u-boo
Biddee bay bee
Bye-bo-boo

Chorus:
   It's just a kooky song.
   You can sing it, too.
   Any consonant will work with
   A E I O U.

B-a-bay
B-e-bee
B-i-biddee bye
B-o-bo
Biddee bye bo
B-u-boo
Biddee bay bee
Bye-bo-boo

R-a-ray
R-e-ree
R-i-riddee rye
R-o-ro
Riddee rye ro
R-u-roo
Riddee ray ree
Rye-ro-roo

(Chorus)

W-a-way
W-e-wee
W-i-widdee wye
W-o-wo
Widdee wye wo
W-u-woo
Widdee way wee
Wye-wo-woo

(Chorus)

P-a-pay
P-e-pee
P-i-piddee pye
P-o-po
Piddee pye po
P-u-poo
Piddee pay pee
Pye-po-poo

(Chorus)

Music © 1999 John Archambault and David Plummer

Creative Teaching Press

Create a Kooky Song

Materials
- ✓ "B-A Bay" song (page 15)
- ✓ Fish reproducible (page 19)
- ✓ small "mystery" items (e.g., a pen, button, and crayon)
- ✓ bag
- ✓ scissors
- ✓ magnet tape
- ✓ bowl
- ✓ string
- ✓ paper clip
- ✓ stick or ruler

Invite students to create new verses for "B-A Bay" with new initial consonants. This provides students with a great way to practice manipulating sounds to reinforce phoneme substitution—an essential phonemic-awareness skill. Try one of these fun ways to have students select a letter for a new verse:

- Have all students whose names begin with the same letter stand (e.g., *Jennifer, Julie,* and *Jamal*). Invite the class to sing the song using the sound that starts their names.

- Place several small "mystery" items in a bag. Invite a student to select an object from the bag without peeking. Have students first divide the name of the item into separate sounds (e.g., /p/ /e/ /n/), and then have the class sing the song with the first sound.

- Invite a student to stand before the class and point to a body part (e.g., head). Have the class use the beginning sound of the body part (e.g., /h/) to sing a kooky song. Encourage students to tap that body part to the rhythm of the beat while singing the song.

- Make six copies of the Fish reproducible, cut out the fish, and write a letter of the alphabet on each one. Put a piece of magnet tape on each fish, and place the cutouts in a bowl. Create a "fishing rod" by tying one end of a piece of string to a paper clip and the other to the end of a stick or ruler. Invite students to go "fishing" for the next letter to use in singing "B-A Bay."

Will Any Consonant Do?

Materials
- ✓ Boat reproducible (page 20)
- ✓ Word Families List reproducibles (pages 9–11)
- ✓ Alphabet Cards (pages 12–13)
- ✓ writing paper

Students will differentiate between real and nonsense words while practicing phoneme substitution with this activity. The song "B-A Bay" suggests that "Any consonant will work with A E I O U." Show students that not every consonant works with each word family to create a real word. Pass out a copy of the Boat reproducible to pairs of students. Choose a word family, such as -at, from the Word Families List, and write it on the board. Have students write the letters *a* and *t* in the last two windows of the boat. Distribute a set of Alphabet Cards to each pair of students. Invite partners to try all 21 consonants to create a list of words (e.g., *bat, cat, dat, fat, gat,* and *hat*). Encourage students to record the 21 words on a piece of paper. Have pairs of students review the list to determine which words are real and which are nonsense. Challenge students to try different consonant blends (e.g., *gr, fl,* or *sl*) or begin the activity again with a new word family.

What's in a Name?

Materials
✓ Fish reproducible (page 19)
✓ scissors
✓ large blue construction paper
✓ glue
✓ crayons or markers
✓ chart or butcher paper
✓ index cards
✓ tape

What's in a name? The answer is vowels and consonants. Distribute several copies of the Fish reproducible to each student. Invite students to write each letter of their name on a separate fish. Have them cut out the fish and use the cutouts to spell their name on a large piece of blue construction paper. Have students glue their fish in place and color all the vowel fish one color and all of the consonant fish another color. Extend learning with a graphing activity. To graph the number of vowels in students' names, draw five columns on a sheet of chart or butcher paper, and label them 1 through 5. Ask each student to write his or her name on an index card. Invite students to tape their name card in the column that represents the number of vowels in their name. For example, Jamie attaches her card to the column labeled 3 because her name has three vowels. Ask students questions such as *Which vowel appears most often in the names of students in our class?* Extend the activity by graphing the number of syllables in students' names.

Sink or Swim

Materials
✓ Alphabet Cards (pages 12–13)
✓ Fish reproducible (page 19)
✓ Boat reproducible (page 20)
✓ scissors

Divide the class into small groups, and distribute a set of Alphabet Cards and a copy of the Fish and Boat reproducibles to each group. Have students cut out the five fish from the Fish reproducible. Invite one student from each group to be the "captain" of the boat. Have each captain think of a two- to five-letter "mystery word," such as *sand.* Ask the captain to place the *s, a, n,* and *d* letter cards facedown in spelling order on four of the squares of the Boat reproducible. Invite the other members of each group to guess the letters of the mystery word. When a letter is guessed correctly, the captain turns over the card that reveals the corresponding letter.

When a player guesses a letter that does not appear in the word, the captain hands a fish to the group. If the group collects all five fish before guessing the word, the captain wins and thinks of another word for the group to guess. If the group guesses the mystery word before collecting all five fish, a new captain is selected. The new captain begins the game again with a different mystery word.

To help students guess the mystery words, remind them that
• Every word has at least one vowel.
• Certain consonants sometimes occur together, such as *br, st,* and *cl.*
• A word with a long vowel sometimes features a silent *e* at the end.
• Knowledge of word families promotes word-pattern recognition.

A "Long" Came a Vowel

Materials

✓ Fish reproducible (page 19)

The song "B-A Bay" encourages students to explore long-vowel patterns. Teach students the following couplets:

B-a-bay uses **long a.** *How many* **long a** *words can you say?*

B-e-bee uses **long e.** *How many* **long e** *words can there be?*

B-i-biddee bye uses **long i.** *How many* **long i** *words can you try?*

B-o-bo uses **long o.** *How many* **long o** *words do you know?*

B-u-boo uses **long u.** *How many* **long u** *words will be new?*

Choose one "long vowel of the day," and invite students to name words that feature that long-vowel sound. Write student responses on fish cutouts. Display cutouts on a board or word wall to encourage students to use these words in their writing.

A-E-I-O-U Boat

Materials

✓ Boat reproducible (page 20)
✓ Alphabet Cards (pages 12–13)

Use this activity to teach students the relationship between silent *e* and long vowels and to have students practice phoneme blending and substitution. Distribute a copy of the Boat reproducible to each student. Direct students to write the letter *a* in the third window and the letter *e* in the fifth window. Demonstrate the activity by placing an *r* in the second window and a *t* in the fourth window. Have students sound out the word, /r/ /ā/ /t/. Emphasize that the *e* is not spoken. Cover the *e* and have students blend the new word, /r/ /ā/ /t/. Discuss the effect the vowel *e* has on the vowel *a*. Distribute a set of Alphabet Cards to each student. Invite students to replace the letters *r* and *t* to create new words. Extend the activity by having students replace the *a* with another vowel. Or, challenge students to create five-letter words that begin with a blend or digraph.

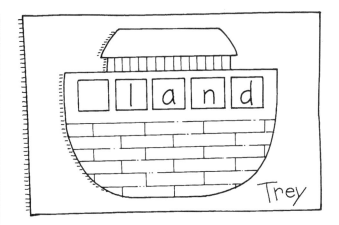

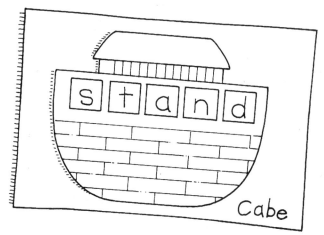

Fish

B-A Bay

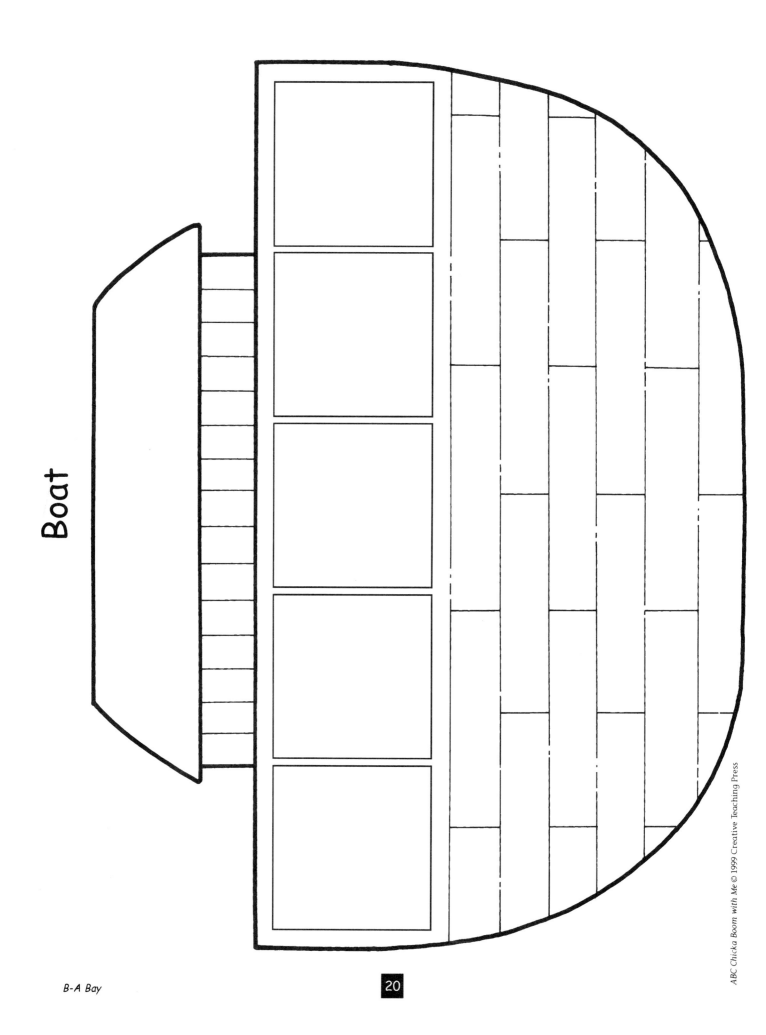

Boat

Braggin' Dragon

One morning early purley,
In my waterlily pad,
A sweet-beat morning
And the sun was shining glad.
I was dreamin' I was taking
A sleepy-day vacation,
When I heard my mama coming
Spitting fire and thunderation.

"You're not sick. I know that trick.
You're not fooling me.
So trim your wick for school, quick,
And the dragon spelling-bee."

"Ho hum, Mom, let me show you
    some.
It's a d-r-a with a g-o-n.
So ta-ta-toodle and good-bye, Mom.
I'm a whizkid speller.
School here I come."

So off I go—
A dynamo on my roller-skatin'
    wheels.
With a d-r-a and a g-o-n—
Slicker than banana peels.

My ten-speed gears up
Twice as fast—
D-r-a down rabbit pass.
And g-o-n like a bird can fly.
Dragon-fast, I glide right by.

Shooting like an arrow,
I'm turning up the flame—
Fleeing, skiing, to dragon fame.
I'm faster d-r then the sun a-g-o-n—
Master dragon, number one.

I pop a wheely and make it fly.
I Superman-it through the sky.
Getting to school, just in time,
To take my place in the spelling-bee
    line.

"Spell dragon."
"Dragon? Dragon.
Let me see.
It's n-o-g—a-r-d."

And, when the principal calls me in,
I'll say "Uh, huh. You're right. I win."
This braggin' dragon won the
    backward-bee.
Won't mom and dad be proud of
    me?

And, yea, dear Mom, the loving cup
I give to you to cheer you up.

And now I'll pogo-go-go-go-go-go-go-
    go-away
To celebrate this braggin' dragon day.

Uh, huh. Oh, yea. Gotta go.
See you later. Bye-bye. I'm outta here.

Creative Teaching Press

Whiz Kid Spellers

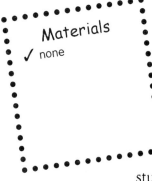

The dragon in "Braggin' Dragon" uses a pattern to remember how to spell: "It's a d-r-a with a g-o-n." Develop a list of other six-letter words, such as *little, school, marker,* and *butter,* and invite students to use the dragon's pattern to spell them (e.g., *I can spell little. It's a l-i-t with a t-l-e* or *I can spell school. It's a s-c-h with an o-o-l*). Invite students to move (e.g., jump, jump, jump, clap, jump, jump, jump) as they spell (e.g., *l-i-t with a t-l-e*). For an extension of the activity, have students make patterns for words of different lengths (e.g., *I can spell party. It's a p and an a and an r-t-y* or *I can spell dog. First a d and then o-g*), and encourage them to move as they clap.

Braggin' Dragon Backward Bee

Place Alphabet Cards for a word in reverse order in a pocket chart, and invite students to guess the correct word. Try *tah* or *ekac.* For extra fun and practice with phoneme segmentation, ask students to sound out the word as it appears backwards before having them guess the correct word. Continue the fun by declaring a "Backwards Day." Encourage students to wear their clothes backwards to school, say the Pledge of Allegience at the end of the day, sit facing the back of the class, write names backwards on papers, and call each other by last names.

Turning up the Flame Game

Materials
✓ Word Families List reproducibles (pages 9–11)

This game uses rhythm and rhyme to help prepare students to read. Divide the class into two teams. Line each team up on either side of the room. Ask one team to select a word from the Word Families List, such as *king,* and have these students move to a beat (e.g., step to the right, clap, step to the left, clap) as they sing this variation of a verse from "Braggin' Dragon":

Shooting like an arrow,
We're turning up the flame.
King *is the word.*
What sounds the same?

Ask the other team to reply with a rhyming word:

Shooting like an arrow,
We're turning up the flame.
Sing *is a word that sounds the same.*

The first team responds with a rhyme for *sing.* Have students continue until all possibilities for that word family have been exhausted. Invite the second team to choose another word from the Word Families List to begin a new round.

Addin' Dragons

Materials
✓ Dragon reproducible (page 25)
✓ yellow butcher paper
✓ scissors
✓ marker

Cover a bulletin board with yellow butcher paper. Cut out several copies of the Dragon reproducible. Fold the wings together over the body. Use a bold marker to write a simple addition problem across the folded wings and write the sum on the belly. Place the dragons on a bulletin board under the title *Addin' Dragons.* Have students solve each problem before opening the dragon's wings to reveal the solution. For a variation, feature simple subtraction problems.

Dragon Detectives

Photocopy a Dragon reproducible for each student. Have students work with a partner. Assign a pair of rhyming words from the song (e.g., *trick/quick, me/bee, fly/sky*) to each pair. Write each rhyming word on a separate dragon, and tape one to each partner's back. (The student should not see the word on his or her own back.) Encourage partners to help each other guess the word on their back by having them give each other rhyming words as clues. For example, a student wearing a dragon with the word *fly* could be given the clues *try, my, why,* and *tie.* Have students play until all have identified their word.

Materials

✓ Dragon reproducible (page 25)
✓ tape

Thinkin' Dragons

Materials

✓ drawing paper
✓ crayons or markers
✓ bookbinding materials

The Braggin' Dragon is certainly a clever character. Invite students to highlight some of his feats. The following activities will allow students to demonstrate that they are just as inventive!

• Ask students to describe the abilities of a dragon, such as breathes fire and flies with wings. Invite students to generate a list of places a dragon might or might not decide to go because of these characteristics. Examples of places a dragon might go include a barbecue or a campfire. Places a dragon might not want to go include an ice-cream parlor or a wax museum. Have individual students illustrate these silly images to share with the class.

• Although it isn't polite to brag, it is important to be proud of your accomplishments. Invite students to describe something they can do well, such as ride a bike or play the piano. Have students use words or pictures to explain their achievements, and bind the pages together in a book titled *Our Braggin' Book.*

• Challenge students to name the different ways the dragon says good-bye at the end of the song. Explain that these are all synonyms for *good-bye.* Encourage students to find words for *farewell* in other languages.

Dragon

Braggin' Dragon

Chicka Chicka Funk

A told B and B told C,
"I'll meet you at the top of the coconut tree."
"Whee," said D to E, F, G,
"I'll beat you to the top of the coconut tree."
Chicka chicka boom boom.
Will there be enough room?

Here comes H up the coconut tree.
And I and J and tag-along K—
All on their way up the coconut tree.
Chicka chicka boom boom.
Will there be enough room?

Look who's coming—it's L, M, N, O, P.
And Q, R, S and T, U, V.
Chicka chicka boom boom.
Will there be enough room?

Still more —W.
Still more —W and X, Y, Z.
The whole alphabet's up the . . .
Oh! No!
Chicka chicka boom boom!

Chicka chicka boom boom.
Chicka chicka boom boom.
Chicka chicka boom boom boom boom.
Chicka chicka boom boom.

Creative Teaching Press

Lyrics © 1999 John Archambault Music © 1999 John Archambault and David Plummer

ABC Adventures

Invite students to use the alphabet and the rhyming pattern in the first couplet of "Chicka Chicka Boom Boom" to create new couplets. Choose a theme, such as food, and invite the class to brainstorm a list of foods that begin with *a*, *b*, and *c*. Choose one word from the list for each letter, and fill in the couplet frame at right. Invite students to brainstorm a rhyming word or phrase for the word to complete the second line of the couplet. Have students use ABC books from the Literature Links (see page 64) for ideas.

Apple told **banana** and **banana** told **cantaloupe,**

"I'll meet you at the top by **climbing a rope.***"*

Have students continue the food theme with the remaining letters of the alphabet, or encourage students to choose other themes, such as names, animals, or clothing, to create couplets. Extend the activity by having students work together in small groups to write the couplets and illustrate them. Bind the pages together into a class book titled *ABC Adventures.*

Word Family Trees

This activity helps students use patterns in rhyming words to spell new words. Draw a coconut tree on a piece of butcher paper and post it. Photocopy several coconuts from the Coconut reproducible and cut them out. Choose a set of words from the Word Families List. Select one word, such as *mop*, and write it on the trunk of the tree. Invite the class to name words that rhyme with *mop*. Write each rhyming word on a coconut cutout, tape it to the top of the tree, and invite the whole class to respond by singing the following verse to the tune of "Chicka Chicka Funk." Replace the first bolded word in the last line with the students' suggestions.

Chicka chicka boom boom.
Better make some more room.
Hop *is a word that rhymes with* **mop.**

Encourage students to use words from the list in their own writing. Repeat the activity on another day with a different word family, such as *-at* or *-ip.*

Coconut Game

Materials
✓ Alphabet Cards (pages 12–13)

This activity provides a fun way for students to practice discriminating between vowels and consonants. Divide the class into pairs, and distribute a set of Alphabet Cards to each pair. Have students shuffle the Alphabet Cards and place them facedown in a pile. The first player selects a card. If the letter is a vowel, the student takes another turn. If the letter is a consonant, play continues with the next person. The first player to collect ten consonant cards wins.

Chicka Chicka March

Materials
✓ Coconuts reproducible (page 30)
✓ chairs
✓ scissors

This variation of "Musical Chairs" gives students practice responding to the rhythm of a song and matching sounds. Place one chair for each student in a circle. Cut out each coconut on the Coconuts reproducible, and choose five letters of the alphabet. Write each letter on a cutout, and place each one on a different chair. Invite students to march in a circle around the chairs to the beat of the song "Chicka Chicka Funk." Tell students to sit in the chair closest to them when the music stops. Play and stop the song at random. Invite those students who are sitting on a coconut cutout to stand and recite a word that begins with their letter. For example, the student with the *n* coconut could say *night*. Try one of these variations of the game:

• Require student answers to feature the sound the letter makes in either the middle or at the end of a word.

• Use more letters or use one coconut cutout for each student.

• Write a word from the Word Families List on each coconut cutout, and have students name a word that rhymes with it.

Tag-Along K

Materials

✓ Jamaica Tag-Along by Juanita Hill

✓ Alphabet Cards (pages 12–13)

✓ writing paper

The letter *K* is called the "tag-along" in "Chicka Chicka Boom Boom." Try one of these activities that incorporate the tag-along theme to have students practice phoneme blending, spelling, and writing skills.

• Explain that *k* often tags along with *c* or *n* to create one sound. Have students generate lists of words that feature either /ck/, as in *tack, sick, sock,* and *luck,* or /nk/, as in *bank, sink, sunk,* and *honk.* Ask students to think of other letters that tag along with each other, such as *p* and *h, t* and *h,* or *s* and *t.* Have students brainstorm lists of words for these sounds as well.

• Arrange students in a circle, and distribute an Alphabet Card to each child. (If there are less than 26 students, give students more than one card.) Announce a word, such as *sun,* and point to the student holding the card that corresponds with the first letter of the word. Have the student with *s* then tag the student holding the next letter in the word. Ask the students to form a "train" and travel to find the third letter. When all of the letters are in place, ask the members of the train to make the sound of their letter (e.g., /s/ /u/ /n/). Invite the class to blend the sounds to say the word *sun.* Have the tag-along train take a trip around the circle before having students repeat the activity with a new word.

• Introduce students to another tag-along in the story *Jamaica Tag-Along.* Have students tell or write about a time that they wanted to tag along with someone else or someone else wanted to tag along with them.

What Lives in Trees?

Materials

✓ drawing paper

✓ crayons or markers

Invite students to brainstorm a list of animals that live in trees, such as *birds, monkeys,* and *squirrels.* Have each student illustrate one example from the list. Call on individual students to hold up their drawing, and invite the class to sound out the name of the animal. Encourage the class to imitate the sound and actions the animal makes. As an alternative to this activity, have students explore fruits that grow on trees.

/b/ /i/ /r/ /d/

Chicka Chicka Funk

Coconuts

Chicka Chicka Funk

ABC Chicka Boom with Me © 1999 Creative Teaching Press

We Are Hippopotamus

We are hippopotamus.
There's really not a lot of us.
We love to go a-wading in the wiver.

When the weather gets quite hot,
We've got a shady little spot,
With lots of mud to cool our blood
And make us quiver.

Wolling in the mud, mud, mud.
Rolling cools our blood, blood, blood.

We are hippopotamus.
There's really not a lot of us.
We love to go a-rolling in the
Mud, mud, mud, muddy-mud.
In the mud, mud, mud, muddy-mud.
Mud, mud.

Oh, we slop in the slud.
We squish in the squud.
We stroll, we skip, and we slish in the splud.
Wolling and wallowing,
We wuv what we do
When the wiver gets muddy.
Woo, woo. Woo, woo.

Oh, we slop in the slud.
We squish in the squud.
We stroll, we skip, and we slish in the splud.
Wolling and wallowing,
We wuv what we do
When the wiver gets muddy.
Woo, woo. Woo, woo.

Lyrics and Music © 1999 David Plummer

Creative Teaching Press

Weather or Not

Materials
✓ butcher paper
✓ crayons or markers

When the weather gets too hot, you can be sure to find the hippos hiding in the mud. But what about other kinds of weather? Invite students to brainstorm different types of weather, including rainy, sunny, cloudy, breezy, hazy, stormy, and blustery. Have small groups of students replace the bolded rhyming words in the following lines from "We Are Hippopotamus" to show what a hippo might do in different climates: *When the weather gets quite **hot**,/We've got a shady little **spot**.* For example, students might write *When the weather isn't **cool**,/We find a big wet swimming **pool*** or *When the weather looks like **snow**,/It's off to the slopes we **go**.* Have small groups of students describe and illustrate one of their couplets on butcher paper, and display the pictures around the classroom.

Julia

Shady Spot

Materials
✓ Alphabet Cards (pages 12–13)
✓ chart paper

The second verse of "We Are Hippopotamus" features words from the -ot word family. Have students practice phoneme substitution by having them change the onset of the word *spot* in the line "We've got a shady little spot." Distribute a set of Alphabet Cards to each student Have students place the letters *o* and *t* on a table, and encourage them to experiment with different consonants to form new words, such as *pot, dot,* and *cot.* Challenge students to rewrite the line with the new -ot word and an adjective that describes it. For example, students might write *We've got a **shiny** little **pot**, We've got a **tiny** little **dot**,* or *We've got a **comfy** little **cot**.* Write the sentences on chart paper, and read them together as a class.

Bath Math

Incorporate this activity into a morning calendar routine. Cut out a copy of the Hippopotamus reproducible, and write a number on the hippo's back. Hold up the cutout as you recite the following verse:

*I love this hippo. She's my **buddy**.*
*But whenever I see her she is awfully **muddy**.*
*It has been **seven** days since she's taken a **bath**.*
*What day was that? You do the **math!***

Challenge students to use the class calendar to determine the last day the hippo took a bath. Suggest various strategies for solving the problem, such as counting backwards or using fingers and other manipulatives. Change the number in the verse for each new calendar session. Extend the activity by writing verses for other parts of the hippo's day. For example:

*I love this hippo. She's really **neat**.*
*But whenever I see her she wants to **eat**.*
*It has been **three** days since she's eaten **lunch**.*
*When was the last time she sat down to **munch**?*

Muddy Buddies

Enlarge eight copies of the Hippopotamus reproducible, and staple them to a light-blue butcher paper background on a board under the title *Muddy Buddies*. Create eight "mud puddles" from brown or black construction paper.

Select eight pairs of rhyming words from the Word Families List. Write one word from each pair on a hippopotamus and the other word on a mud puddle. Staple the hippos to the board. Place the puddles at the bottom of the board. Invite students to match each puddle with the rhyming hippopotamus. A variation of this board would be to feature words on the puddles that begin with the same onsets as the words on the hippos (e.g., *ball* and *bet*).

We Are Hippopotamus

Wading in the Wolling Wiver

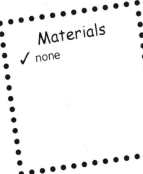

Materials
- ✓ Hippopotamus reproducible (page 35)
- ✓ crayons or markers

Discuss with the class examples of places where the /r/ and /w/ are interchanged in "We Are Hippopotamus." Teach students the verse at right that uses images from the song. Invite students to replace the bolded letters with the first letter of their name to create a silly rhyme. Make up motions to accompany the verse.

Verse	Motion
Quiver, quiver, shake and shiver,	Fold arms over chest and shiver with the cold.
Making rhymes is in our blood.	Clap for each word.
*Bill goes **b**ading in the **b**iver.*	Take large steps for each word as if wading in water.
*Bill goes **b**olling in the **b**ud.*	Turn in place as if rolling in mud.

Encourage each student to write a verse that features his or her name on a copy of the Hippopotamus reproducible. Have students decorate and share their verse with other students.

Russ the Hippopotamus

Materials
- ✓ none

Play this version of the game "Concentration" to give students practice matching sounds and isolating phonemes. Invite students to sit cross-legged in a circle. Have students slap their knees, clap their hands, snap their right hand, and snap their left hand as an accompaniment to the following verse:

> *Please meet Russ*
> *The Hippopotamus,*
> *And listen to the sounds in his name.*
> */P/ is one.*
> *Let's have some fun.*
> *Think of some words that start with the same.*

Point to a student to give an example of a /p/ word, such as *pencil*, during the "slap knees" portion of the sequence. Repeat the process with the next student in the circle until no more /p/ words can be named. Substitute the position and/or name of the sound in the verse frame with another to begin the game again.

Hippopotamus

We Are Hippopotamus

The Happapatamus

A long time ago,
In a land far away,
Lived a very large creature without a name.

He looked rather sad,
His eyes kinda glum,
Because he didn't have a name and he knew no one.

He was a H A P P A P A T A M U S. No! No!
He was a H E P P E P E T A M U S. No! No!
He was a H I P P I P I T A M U S. No! No!
He was a H O P P O P O T A M U S. No! No!
He was a H U P P U P U T A M U S. No! No!

He was a H-I-P-P-O—Hippo.
He was a H-I-P-P-O-P-O-T.
He was a H-I-P-P-O-P-O-T-A.
He was a H-I-P-P-O-P-O-T-A-M-U-S.
He's a Hip-po-pot-a-mus. Yes! Yes!

He was a H-I-P-P-O—Hippo.
He was a H-I-P-P-O-P-O-T.
He was a H-I-P-P-O-P-O-T-A.
He was a H-I-P-P-O-P-O-T-A-M-U-S.
He's a Hip-po-pot-a-mus. Yes! Yes!

Lyrics and Music © 1999 John Archambault and David Plummer

But Not the Hippopotamus

Read aloud *But Not the Hippopotamus* to students. This delightful story uses clever rhymes to tell of a shy hippo who terribly wants to join the other animals as they try new things. Review the rhymes in the story with students, and have them create new ones. Display lines from the book on chart paper, and challenge students to change the underlined parts. For example:

Original:	A bear and hare <u>have been to the fair.</u>
New Version:	A bear and hare <u>climbed up a stair.</u>
Original:	A cat and two rats are <u>trying on hats.</u>
New Version:	A cat and two rats are <u>sitting on mats.</u>

Invite students to work in small groups. Assign one page of the story to each group to rewrite and illustrate. Bind the pages together, and title the book *But Not Our Hippopotamus*. Extend the activity by having students write about a time they felt left out. Invite students to illustrate their stories and share them with the class.

He Was a What?

The Happapatamus had to go through all five vowels before figuring out his name. Explore this pattern in the song. Invite students to work with a partner to experiment with the name of another animal. Have partners write the animal's name five different ways, each time changing one or more vowels to either *a, e, i, o,* or *u*. Encourage students to illustrate their animal and then exchange papers with another pair. Challenge students to determine which of the five words is spelled correctly. Use the lyrics of the song to guide students with the appropriate spelling.

alaphant
elephant
iliphant
olophant
uluphant

Ben

The Happapatamus

Spelling Stairs

Materials

✓ "The Happapatamus" song (page 36)
✓ Word Families List reproducibles (pages 9–11)
✓ overhead transparency
✓ overhead projector

Tell students that the best way for the Happapatamus to learn to pronounce and spell his new name was to break it down into parts. Make an overhead transparency of the lyrics to "The Happapatamus," and place it on an overhead projector to help students explore the spelling technique in the last verse. Have students use the following stair format to spell words from the class spelling list or the Word Families List:

h
ha
hat

Try having students clap or jump for each letter as it is said. Invite students to use this technique to spell their names or vocabulary words.

Hello, Hippo!

Materials

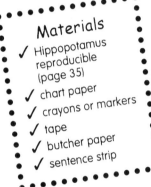

✓ Hippopotamus reproducible (page 35)
✓ chart paper
✓ crayons or markers
✓ tape
✓ butcher paper
✓ sentence strip

The Happapatamus was lost without a name and friends. Invite students to tell about a time they felt lonely. The following poem describes how one hippopotamus feels. Write the poem on chart paper, and tape a decorated copy of the Hippopotamus reproducible beside it. Invite students to read the poem aloud.

*This hippo looks **sad.***
*This hippo looks **glum.***
*This hippo has no name and knows no **one.***
*This hippo has a favor to ask of **you.***
*"Give me a name and a few friends, **too!"***

Pass out a copy of the Hippopotamus reproducible to each student. Invite students to give the glum guy a new alliterative name, such as "Happy Heart Hippo." Provide time for students to "introduce" their hippo to the hippo friends of other students. Invite small groups of students (and their hippos) to work together. Give each group a large sheet of butcher paper. Have the groups use words and pictures to tell about the things that their hippo friends like to do together. Challenge students to use the rhyme pattern from the poem to tell a story like the following:

*These hippos are **glad.***
*They like to have **fun.***
*They play all day in the bright warm **sun.***
*There's one more thing that they like to **do—***
*They hide behind trees and play **peek-a-boo!***

Display murals under a sentence strip with the words *Hippo Hippo Hooray!* written on it.

Hip-O-Pot-Toe-Miss

Teach students the jump-rope rhyme "Hip-O-Pot-Toe-Miss" to help them practice splitting syllables. Lead the class to a large, open area, and demonstrate the following motions for students to mimic while jumping a rope that is turned by two volunteers:

Hip   Hands on **hips.**
O   Clasp hands and raise arms above head to create an **o.**
Pot   Move clasped hands down to waist level to create a **pot.**
Toe   Touch **toes.**
Miss   Stop jumping to **miss** the rope.

Have students try breaking down other words (e.g., *elevator* or *alligator*) into syllables while jumping rope.

He Was a What?

Teach students the following verse:
Gus, Gus, the hippopotamus.
*   Went to school on a big yellow bus.*
*   The driver made a great big fuss*
*   To have a hippo ride on the bus.*

Invite small groups of students to create new verses with different animals. For example:

Gar, Gar, the fierce jaguar,
Went to school in a little red car.
Everyone thought he was such a star
To ride to school in a little red car.

Have students try other animals, such as "Brant, Brant, the grey elephant" or "Jake, Jake, the long, slithery snake." Add *How many blocks did he ride?* to the end of the verse and you have a great jump-rope rhyme. The number of blocks equals the number of jumps a student makes before missing.

Alphabet Zoo

Alligator	Buffalo	Camel	Dolphin,
Elephant	Fox	Gorilla	Hippopotamus,
Iguana	Jaguar	Koala	Lion,
Moose	Numbat	Otter	Parrot,
Quail	Raccoon	Seal and	Tiger,
Umbrella bird	Vulture	Walrus	X-ray fish,
Yak and	Zebra.		

All the animals in my alphabet zoo, zoo, zoo.
All the animals in my alphabet zoo.

(Repeat)

I want to see all the animals—
All the animals in my alphabet zoo.

I want to see all the animals—
All the animals in my alphabet zoo, zoo, zoo.
All the animals in my alphabet zoo.

Lyrics and Music © 1999 John Archambault and David Plummer

The Name Game

This is the Name Game.
Go through the alphabet
    and say your name.
A my name is Amy.
B my name is Burt.
C my name is Cathy, and I
    dig in the dirt.

D my name is Danielle.
E my name is Eric.
F my name is Frank, and it
    rhymes with Hank.

G my name is Gail.
H my name is Hannah.
I my name is Irene.
J my name is Jack like Jack
    and Jill.

K my name is Karen.
L my name is Laura.
M my name is Mike, and I
    ride my bike.

N my name is Nancy.
O my name is Omar.
P my name is Paula. I'm
    from O-hi-o.

Q my name is Quinten.
R my name is Robin.
S my name is Sam.
T my name is Teresa. I like
    jelly and jam.

U my name is Ursulla.
V my name is Vick.
W my name is Wanda. I
    like Willy Wonka and
    his chocolate factory.

X my name is Xavier.
Y my name is Yolanda.
Z my name is Zack.

This is the Name Game.
Go through the alphabet
    and say your name.

Lyrics and Music © 1999 John Archambault and David Plummer

Creative Teaching Press

Animal Card Code

Turn a day at the zoo into a mystery game, and have students practice sound-matching skills at the same time. Ask a student or two to visit a place outside of your classroom. Invite the remaining students to suggest a word that uses only the letters *a, b, c, e, g, i, n, o, p, s, t,* and *u.* (These are the first letters of the twelve animals that appear on the Animal Cards. Make several sets of the Animal Cards available for use in this activity.) Use the Animal Cards to "spell" the words. For example, for the word *pets,* post the **p**arrot, **e**lephant, **t**iger, and **s**eal cards on the board. Call student volunteers back into the room. Invite these students to identify the mystery word by having them sound out the first letter of each animal name on the card and then blend the sounds together (e.g., /p/ /e/ /t/ /s/). Repeat the activity a few more times with the whole class. Give small groups of students their own sets of Animal Cards, and encourage them to create their own mystery words using "animal card code."

Feeding Time at the Zoo

It's feeding time at the "Alphabet Zoo." Have students practice matching sounds and putting words into alphabetical order while the animals enjoy a tasty treat.

Name an animal in the zoo, and invite students to think of a food that begins with the same sound as the first letter of the animal's name (e.g., an apple for the alligator). Write student ideas on chart paper. Have students sing the new words to the tune of "Alphabet Zoo":

Alligator **apples**
Buffalo **bananas**
Camel **coconuts**
Dolphin **doughnuts**

*All the animals in our alphabet zoo, zoo, zoo
Like to eat the same foods that you do.*

*We want to feed all the animals,
All the animals in our alphabet zoo.*

Invite each student to illustrate an animal eating an alphabet treat on a copy of the Habitat reproducible. Extend the activity by changing *We want to feed all the animals* to *We want to be all the animals.* Encourage students to imitate the animals named in the song "Alphabet Zoo."

Where, Oh Where, Could Those Animals Be?

Materials
- ✓ "Alphabet Zoo" song (page 40)
- ✓ index cards
- ✓ large envelope

Invite students to discover which animals are hiding in the Alphabet Zoo. Have a small group of students play this game upon finishing work early or during a free-choice period. Write the names of each of the 26 animals from the song "Alphabet Zoo" on a separate index card. Remove a few of these cards at random before placing the set in a large envelope. Explain to students that a few animals are "hiding" in the zoo, and invite them to determine which animals are missing. Suggest students put the cards into alphabetical order as a strategy for determining which creatures have gone "undercover."

What the Animals Do at the Zoo

Materials
- ✓ Habitat reproducible (page 46)
- ✓ Animal Cards reproducible (page 45)
- ✓ scissors
- ✓ crayons or markers
- ✓ glue
- ✓ stapler
- ✓ construction paper

Invite students to think about some of the ways animals spend their day at the zoo. Have students practice critical-thinking and phoneme-substitution skills as they create individual books. Make five copies of the Habitat reproducible. Write each of the following lines in the banner on a separate page:

Page 1   *The ___ takes a bath every ___* **ay.**
Page 2   *Listen to what the _____ have to ___* **ay.**
Page 3   *Watch how the _____ ___* **ay.**
Page 4   *Where are the _____? The sign shows the ___* **ay.**
Page 5   *At night, this is where the _____ ___* **ay.**

Photocopy a set of the revised pages for each student. Pass out a set of revised pages and a set of Animal Cards to each student. Invite students to fill in the first blank in each sentence with an animal featured in the set of cards. Ask students to write an onset that completes the rhyme in the second blank. For example:

> *The **elephant** takes a bath every **day**.*
> *Listen to what the **lions** have to **say**.*
> *Watch how the **gorillas play**.*
> *Where are the **otters**? The sign shows the **way**.*
> *At night, this is where the **tigers lay**.*

Encourage students to make their own drawings or use pictures cut from the Animal Cards to illustrate the sentences on each page. Have each student staple all five pages together under a construction-paper cover and write the title *What Animals Do at the Zoo* on the cover.

43

Playing the Name Game

Try one of these different ways to get students involved in singing "The Name Game":

• Invite students to use their classmates' names as they go through the alphabet.

• Introduce a geography lesson by challenging students to think of cities, towns, states, and countries that start with the first letter of their name (e.g., *A my name is Amy and I'm from* **Albany** *or B my name is Burt and I'm from* **Boston**). Have students use maps or an atlas as a resource to identify and locate the names of these places. Make a list of cities, towns, states, and countries as a reference for younger students.

• Have students jump rope while singing "The Name Game."

ABC, an Animal, and Me

Use this activity to reinforce sound-matching skills and teach students about active verbs. Explain that the children mentioned in "The Name Game" take a trip to the Alphabet Zoo. Invite each student to change the bolded parts of the couplet to words that begin with the same sound as the first letter of their name (e.g., *A my name is* **Andrea.** *I* **pick apples** *with the* **alligator**). Invite students to write their couplet on the banner of the Habitat reproducible and illustrate the couplet with a silly image in the space provided. Bind the pages together into a book, and title it *ABC, an Animal, and Me.*

A my name is Andrea. I pick apples with the alligator.

Animal Cards

alligator	buffalo	camel
elephant	gorilla	iguana
numbat	otter	parrot
seal	tiger	umbrella bird

45

Habitat

Jump Rope Rhymes

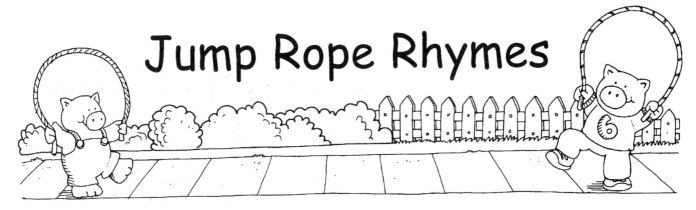

Lyrics adapted by John Archambault Music © 1999 John Archambault and David Plummer

One, two, buckle my shoe.
Three, four, shut the door.
Five, six, pick up sticks.
Seven, eight, lay them straight.
Nine, ten, a big fat hen.
Nine, ten, here we go again.

Rhythm, rhythm—
Gotta have a beat.
Snap your fingers and
Stomp your feet.
Clap your hands and
Slap your knee.
That's called rhythm.
Don't you see!

Let's get the rhythm of the fingers.
Snap, snap.
Let's get the rhythm of the hands.
Clap, clap.
Let's get the rhythm of the knees.
Knock, knock.
Let's get the rhythm of the feet.
Stomp, stomp.

Rhythm, rhythm—
Gotta have a beat.
Snap your fingers and
Stomp your feet.
Clap your hands and
Slap your knee.
That's called rhythm.
Don't you see!

My mother, your mother
Live across the street—
1819 Mulberry Street.
When they get to talking,
This is what they say,
"Boys go to Jupiter to loop the Lupiter.
Girls go to college to get more knowledge."

Icky, icky, soda pop.
Icky, icky, poo.
Icky, icky, soda pop.
I love you.

Chicka, chicka, whole potata.
Half past allagata.
Bim, bam, bolagata.
Give three cheers
For the dippy, dappy, happy, sappy readers.
Are we happy?
Well, I guess.
Readers. Readers.
Yes. Yes. Yes.

Pennies in my pocket
Jingle jangle with my keys.
Peanuts in my pocket—
Feed the elephants please.
Picked a periwinkle
At the zoo.
Put it in my pocket with my popcorn, too.
And my peanut butter sandwich—
I saved half for you.
Put my hand in
To pull it all out—
Sticky, icky.
Hear my mama shout,
"Take your pants off.
Pull your pockets inside-out."

Rhythm, rhythm—
Gotta have a beat.
Snap your fingers and
Stomp your feet.
Clap your hands and
Slap your knee.
That's called rhythm.
Don't you see!

Creative Teaching Press

Rhythm, Rhythm, Gotta Have a Beat

Materials
✓ jump ropes
✓ triangles, rhythm sticks, maracas, and other simple instruments

This song promotes the three Rs of learning—rhyme, rhythm, and repetition. Have students practice important phonemic-awareness skills while they enjoy the strong beat, silly rhymes, and repetitive phrasing of "Jump Rope Rhymes." Have students jump rope to the song or try one of these exciting rhythm activities:

• Have students clap hands or use other simple instruments, such as triangles, rhythm sticks, and maracas, to express the rhythm of the song.

• Ask students to sing the song using different voices or tones. Invite them to experiment with one of the following examples or make up others: high pitch, low pitch, "stuffy nose," "underwater," yodel, staccato.

• Divide the class into four groups. Have each group keep the rhythm simultaneously with one of the following movements in the song: snap, clap, knee slap, and foot stomp.

Nine, Ten, Here We Go Again

Materials
✓ chart paper
✓ drawing paper
✓ crayons or markers

Reverse the count in the first verse of the song. Write the numeral words on chart paper, and invite the class to complete the rhymes. For example:

Ten, nine, *a baby's whine.*
Eight, seven, *my cousin Kevin.*
Six, five, *a tricky hand jive.*
Four, three, *climb a tree.*
Two, one, *the bright yellow sun.*

Or, try substituting letters for numbers:
A, B, C, *a stinging bee.*
D E, F, *my brother Jeff.*
G, H, I, *a pumpkin pie.*
J, K, L, *a ringing bell.*

Assign each line to a student or pairs of students to illustrate on drawing paper. Invite the class to sing the new verses together. Have students hold up their artwork when the coordinating line of the song is sung.

Soda Pop Song

Display the lyrics to "Jump Rope Rhymes." Invite the class to create silly alternatives to the verse that starts "Icky, icky, soda pop." Demonstrate how to change the onsets (e.g., **St**icky, **st**icky, soda pop) and rimes (e.g., **I**ppy, **i**ppy, soda pop). Or, have students change the noun (e.g., Icky icky, **gum drop**) to give them practice with parts of speech. Divide the class into small groups. Challenge each group to write a silly verse and create a coordinating movement sequence. Invite students to perform their song-and-dance routines for each other.

Pennies in My Pocket

Get students to take their hands out of their pockets and use them in some hands-on practice with phoneme segmentation. Photocopy the lyrics to "Jump Rope Rhymes" for each student. Invite students to circle all the p words on the list (e.g., *pennies, peanuts, popcorn,* and *periwinkle*). Give each student a copy of the Pocket reproducible and a handful of pennies, peanuts, or popcorn. Invite a student to read a *p* word from the lyrics, such as *pennies*. Say the word together with the class, and then separate the sounds (e.g., /p/ /e/ /n/ /ē/ /s/). Have students place one penny, peanut, or piece of popcorn on the Pocket reproducible for each phoneme they hear (e.g., five peanuts for the word *pennies*). Repeat the activity with other words from the lyrics. Extend learning by creating a list of words that begin with another letter or have students place one object on their pocket for each syllable of the word.

Pocket Pairs

Materials
✓ Pocket reproducible (page 51)
✓ Word Families List reproducibles (pages 9–11)
✓ stapler
✓ sentence strips

Enlarge ten copies of the Pocket reproducible, and staple them on to a bulletin board under the title *Pocket Pairs*. Only staple each copy on three sides to create a pocket. Select ten pairs of rhyming words from the Word Families List. Write one word from each pair on a pocket and the other on a sentence strip. Invite the whole class to gather around the board, and show them one sentence strip. Ask a student to slip the strip into the pocket of the rhyming word (e.g., the strip with *sink* would be placed in the pocket labeled *think*). Invite other students to match each remaining sentence strip with a pocket. Extend the use of this board with the following activities:

• Invite students to write as many rhyming words as they can on sentence strips to place in pockets.

• Write pairs of synonyms or antonyms on the pockets and sentence strips for students to match.

• Print a numeral or draw a quantity of dots (from 1–10) on each pocket. Write simple addition and subtraction problems on sentence strips for students to solve by placing them in the pocket that matches the solution to the problem.

Pocket Books

Materials
✓ Pocket reproducible (page 51)
✓ Alphabet Cards (pages 12–13)
✓ crayons or markers
✓ bookbinding materials

This "pocket book" may not be filled with money, but it does hold some valuable opportunities for students to practice phoneme substitution and creative thinking. Explain to students that they will write a book about things they can carry around in their pockets. Make five copies of the Pocket reproducible. Print the words *My Pocket Book* on the first page, and write one of the following frames on each of the other four pages:

> *My Pet ___og*
> *___am and Bread*
> *A Fat ___at*
> *A Shiny ___ell*

Make a copy of these five revised pocket pages for each child. Distribute the five pocket pages and a set of Alphabet Cards to each student.

Encourage students to manipulate their Alphabet Cards to determine the missing onsets for the rime on each page to create real words (e.g., *My Pet Frog* or *My Pet Dog*). Invite students to fill in the blanks with the appropriate letters. Have students illustrate the pages before binding them together into a book.

Pocket

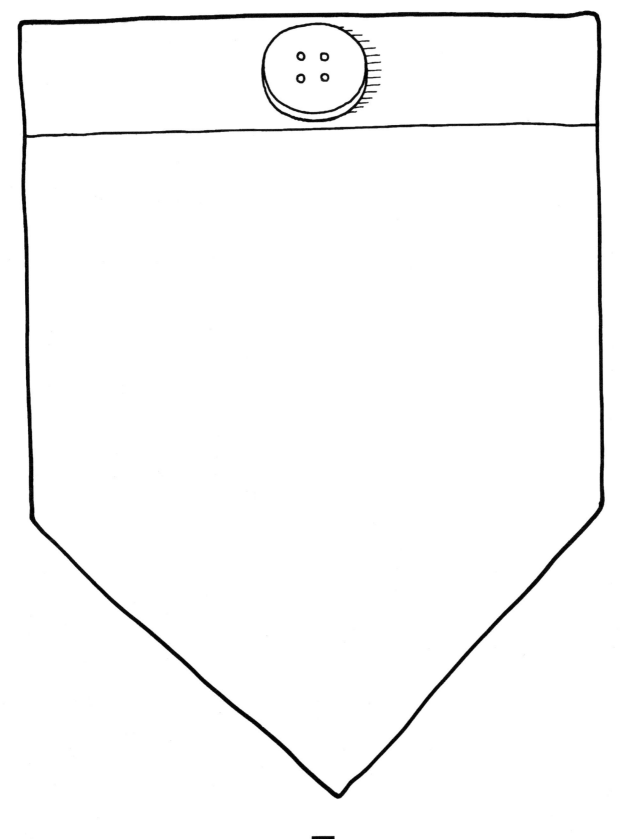

Splish! Splash! Splash!

Splash
Splash splash
Splash splash splash

Splash
Splish splash
Splash splash splash

Sun is shining.
Wind is wailing.
Waves are washing.
Sunday sailing.

Splash
Splash splash
Splash splash splash

Splash
Splish splash
Splash splash splash

Jetski jumping.
Dancing dolphins.
Seagulls singing.
Open ocean.

Splash
Splash splash
Splash splash splash

Splash
Splish splash
Splash splash splash

Surf is swirling.
Splishing, splashing.
Kids canoeing.
River rafting.

Splash
Splash splash
Splash splash splash

Splash
Splish splash
Splash splash splash

Deep-sea diving.
Deep down ocean.
Moon mermaid.
Misty motion.

Whale watching.
Wispy waves.
Whirling, swirling.
Swishing, swaying.

Splash
Splash splash
Splash splash splash

Splash
Splish splash
Splash splash splash

Lyrics and Music © 1999 David Plummer

Splish Splash!

Materials

✓ "Splish! Splash! Splash!" song (page 52)

This song provides the perfect format for having students practice phoneme substitution. Encourage students to try one of these fun ways of singing "Splish! Splash! Splash!" to practice important phonemic-awareness skills.

• Have students change the onset to form real and nonsense words.
> **D**ash
> **D**ish dash
> **D**ash **d**ash **d**ash

• Invite students to experiment with different vowel patterns, both long and short.
> Spl**oo**sh
> Spl**oo**sh spl**oo**sh
> Spl**oo**sh spl**oo**sh spl**oo**sh

• Have students practice breaking words into syllables. Give any three-syllable word, such as *elephant, spaghetti,* or *dinosaur,* and have students try clapping the rhythm of the syllables.
> Di
> Di - no
> Di - no - saur

• Ask students to write simple sentences, and encourage them to use nouns, verbs, and direct objects.
> Joe
> Joe sings.
> Joe sings songs.

Something Fishy

Materials

✓ Fish reproducible (page 19)
✓ scissors
✓ envelopes

Invite the class to determine what is "fishy" about a group of four words. Make a list of four words, three of which have something in common. For example, *sun, fun,* and *run* have the same rhyming pattern. Include a fourth word, such as *sum,* that differs from the first three. Write each of the four words on a fish copied and cut from the Fish reproducible. Invite a student to identify the word that is fishy. Encourage students to explain what is different about the word they identify (e.g., the word *sum* does not rhyme with the other three). To extend the activity, make several sets of "fishy words," and store them in separate envelopes. Place the envelopes in a learning center, and encourage individuals or small groups to identify the different word in each set.

Word Waves

Materials
✓ Wave reproducible (page 56)
✓ Word Families List reproducibles (pages 9–11)
✓ scissors
✓ crayons or markers
✓ tape

Water-related words will roll from the pages of this expandable book project. Give five copies of the Wave reproducible to each student. Invite students to cut out the wave from each page and write the title *Water* on one of them. Have students write and draw pictures to describe a different use for water, such as bathing, swimming, drinking, and cooking, on the remaining four wave pages. Show students how to tape the edges of the waves together and fold them accordion-style, so that the title page is on top. Place finished books in a reading center for students to enjoy.

Vary the activity by having students make a list of five words that rhyme. Have students write each word on a separate page of their "wave book." Invite students to share their list of rhyming words with the class. Ask students to help each other extend the pages of their wave book, one page at a time, while the class reads aloud the rhyming words. Display the "word waves" on the walls of the room to encourage students to use these rhyming words in their writing.

FiSHing SHips

Materials
✓ Boat reproducible (page 20)
✓ Fish reproducible (page 19)
✓ crayons or markers
✓ scissors
✓ glue
✓ large construction paper

Use this activity to help students practice phoneme isolation. Brainstorm with the class a list of words that begin or end with *sh* (e.g., *wish, shut, cash,* and *shower*). Distribute a Boat reproducible and Fish reproducible to each student. Invite students to label their boat with the word *ship* and one fish with the word *fish*. Have students color both their ship and fish before cutting out each one. Show students how to glue their ship to the left side of a piece of construction paper that is positioned vertically. Have students glue their fish to the right side of the paper. Ask students to decide where *sh* appears in each word on the list. Have students write words that begin with *sh*, like *shut* and *shower,* under the ship, and words that end with *sh*, like *wish* and *cash,* under the fish.

ship

shut
shower
show
shine
shoe
shop
shutter

fish

wish
cash
flash
splash
dish
dash
crash

This Splashing Is Simply Smashing

Materials
✓ "Splish! Splash! Splash!" song (page 52)
✓ chart paper

Change the nouns in the third and fifth verses of "Splish! Splash! Splash!" Invite students to substitute the nouns in the sentences (e.g., *Star is shining*). Have students sing the song with the new verses. For example:

Star *is shining.*
Ghost *is wailing.*
Children *are washing.*
Ships *are sailing.*

Have students change the verses by matching sounds with names:

Joanne *is jumping.*
Dayna *is dancing.*
Sue *is singing.*
Oliver *is in the ocean.*

Extend the activity by challenging students to write a whole new song about the class. Change the refrain to "Our busy class." Challenge the class to write alliterative sentences using student names (e.g., *Paula is planting*). For example:

Our Busy Class
Our
Our busy
Our busy class

Paula is planting.
Nicholas is napping.
Emma is eating.
Philip is phoning.

Write the new words on chart paper. Invite students to create simple rhythms (e.g., clap-clap, snap-snap) or movements (e.g., step to the left, clap, step to the right, clap) to perform while singing their song.

55

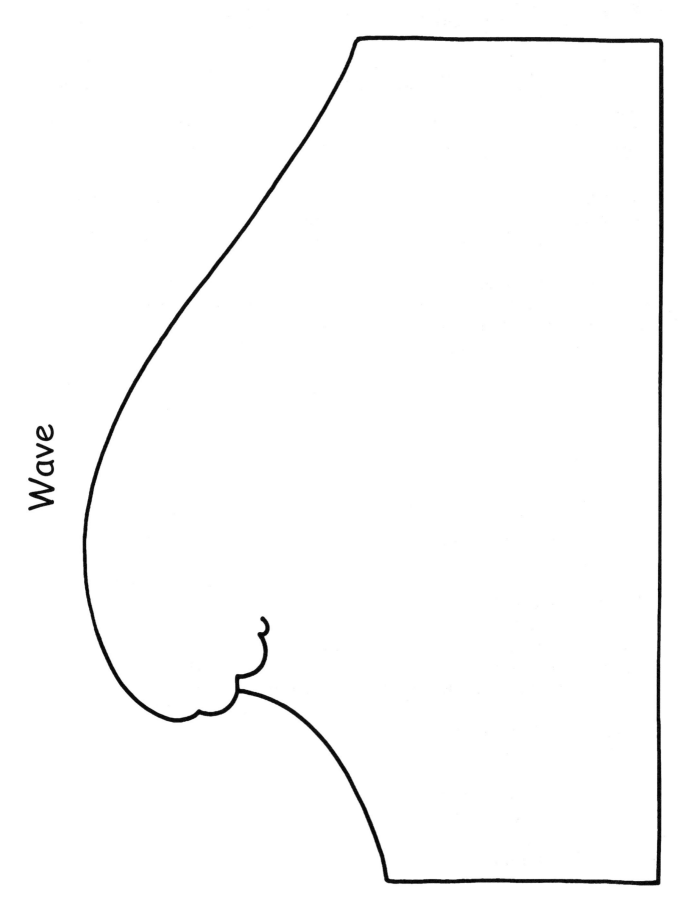

Wave

Splish! Splash! Splash!

ABC Chicka Boom with Me © 1999 Creative Teaching Press

The Long and the Short of It

Five singing vowels put music in
  the words.
A, E, I, O, U—they all want to be
  heard.
Sometimes they'll be shy and
  sometimes they'll be hiding
In between the consonants.
If you look real close you'll find
  them!

Who put the /a/ in Cadillac?
A put the /a/ in Cadillac. Cadillac.
E put the /e/ in elephant.
  Elephant.
I put the /i/ in little pig. Little pig.
O put the /o/ in lollipop. Lollipop.
U put the /u/ in buttercup.
  Buttercup.

But in words like Y-O-U—
What are we to do?
It's a long way around
To make a simple sound.
That's the long and the short of it.

Who put the /ā/ in paper plate?
A put the /ā/ in paper plate. Paper
  plate.
E put the /ē/ in freebie. Freebie.
I put the /ī/ in nice pie. Nice pie.
O put the /ō/ in yo-yo. Yo-yo.
U put the /ū/ in music.

And they say sometimes Y is a
  vowel.
What about this wise guy Y?
He's the shy one.
Yea, there's a Y in fly.
And at the end of good-bye.
Oh my, there's another Y.
But why is there a Y at the start of
  Y-O-U?
That's the long and the short of it.

Five singing vowels put music in
  the words.
A, E, I, O, U—they all want to be
  heard.
Sometimes they'll be shy and
  sometimes they'll be hiding
In between the consonants.
If you look real close you'll find
  them!

In words like Y-O-U—
What are we to do?
It's a long way around
To make a simple sound.
That's the long and the short of it.

Lyrics © 1999 John Archambault Music © 1999 John Archambault and David Plummer

Vowel Vehicles

Materials

✓ Train reproducible (page 61)
✓ Van reproducible (page 62)
✓ Word Families List reproducibles (pages 9–11)
✓ crayons or markers
✓ scissors
✓ tape
✓ chart paper

Spend a few minutes each day on this activity to provide students with practice differentiating between long and short vowels. Explain to students that a long vowel says its own name, like the /ā/ in *train,* and that a short vowel does not say its own name, like the /a/ in *van.* (Help students remember the difference by telling them that a train is longer than a van.) Make a copy of the Train and Van reproducibles. Color and cut out the train and van. Tape the train to the top-left side of a piece of chart paper and the van to the top-right side of the paper. Select a one-syllable word from the Word Families List, and ask students to decide if the vowel they hear in the word is long or short. Write words with a long-vowel sound under the train and words with a short-vowel sound under the van.

cake
light
pole

sit
pot
hum

Putting Music in the Words

Materials

✓ "The Long and the Short of It" song (page 57)
✓ Train reproducible (page 61)
✓ Van reproducible (page 62)
✓ Word Families List reproducibles (pages 9–11)
✓ crayons or markers
✓ scissors
✓ chart paper

Follow one of these suggested activities to help students explore the different ways vowels are heard in words.

• Invite students to change all of the nouns in verses two and four of "The Long and the Short of It" (e.g., *Who put the /a/ in **ham sandwich?** or Who put the /ā/ in **tailgate?**)* and sing the new verses.

• Distribute a copy of the Train and Van reproducibles to each student to color and cut out. Choose one-syllable words from the Word Families List, and write them on chart paper. Have students use the vehicles to identify the vowel sound they hear in each word by asking them to hold up the train for long vowels and the van for short vowels.

The Long and the Short of It

These Words Have Come a LONG Way!

Materials
- ✓ Train reproducible (page 61)
- ✓ Van reproducible (page 62)
- ✓ chart paper
- ✓ crayons or markers
- ✓ scissors
- ✓ paper
- ✓ stapler

Invite students to brainstorm a list of words with a long-vowel sound (e.g., *cake, mice, boat),* and write these words on a piece of chart paper. Ask students to choose one word from the list, and have them write it on a copy of the Train reproducible. Invite students to color and cut out their train car. Give each student a piece of paper, and ask students to draw a picture of their long-vowel word. Staple students' train cutouts in a line on a board under the title *These Words Have Come a LONG Way!* Staple students' drawings above the cars of the train. Extend learning by having students think of words with short vowels. Repeat the activity using the Van reproducible, and change the title of the board to *A Short-Vowel Sound Really Gets Around.*

Wow! What a Vowel

Materials
- ✓ Alphabet Cards (pages 12–13)
- ✓ writing paper

Invite students to write the five vowels down the center of a piece of paper. Distribute the Alphabet Cards for *b, g, n, l, r,* and *t* to each student. Invite students to use two different consonants at one time to create words from the vowels. Show students how to place one consonant card before the vowel and one consonant card after the vowel to create a word. For example, a student uses *b* and *t* to create the word *bat.* Have students slide the two consonant cards down the column to create new words with the other four vowels. Encourage students to write a list of the five new words. Ask students to identify which words are real and which words are nonsense. For example:

b a t	**real word**
b e t	**real word**
b i t	**real word**
b o t	**nonsense word**
b u t	**real word**

The Long and the Short of It

Shy Y, the Wise Guy

Materials
✓ writing paper

The fifth verse of "The Long and Short of It" explores the different sounds associated with the letter *y*. Have students explore why *y* is sometimes "shy" and sometimes a "wise guy." In words like *bay* and *key, y* is shy because only the long vowel is heard. In words like *fly, funny,* and *you, y* is the wise guy because it makes its own sound (i.e., /ī/ in *fly*, /ē/ in *funny*, and /y/ in *you*). Divide the class into small groups. Have students brainstorm as many words as they can that are spelled with the letter *y*, list them on writing paper, and then report their ideas back to the class. Encourage the class to work together to identify the words in which *y* is shy and wise.

Long or Short...You're It!

Materials
✓ none

Play this version of "TV Tag" with small groups of students in a wide open space. Announce a vowel sound, such as long *a*. Select one student to be "it," and have him or her attempt to tag another student. The only protection a student has from being tagged is to sit down and say a word with the long *a* sound, such as *late*. A student who is tagged before naming a long *a* word becomes "it." Change the vowel sound to extend the fun and learning.

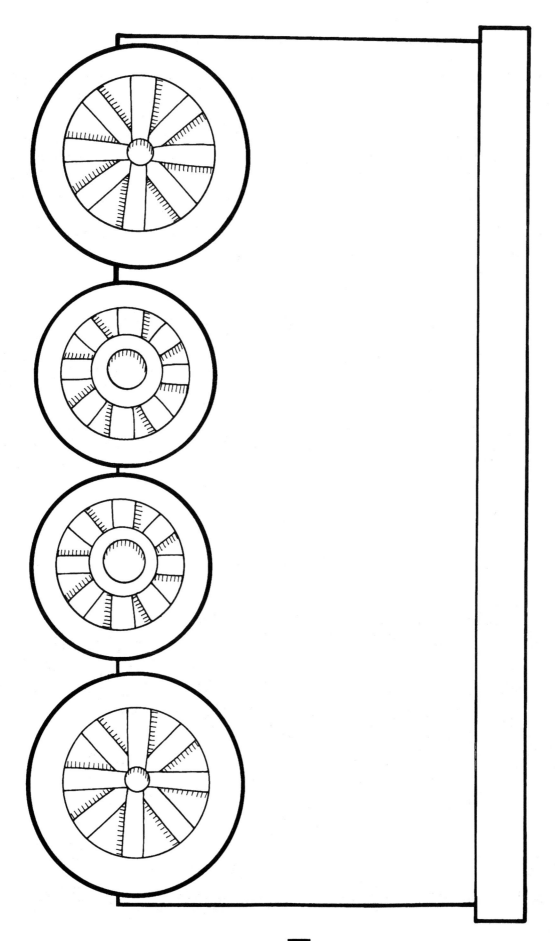

Train

The Long and the Short of It

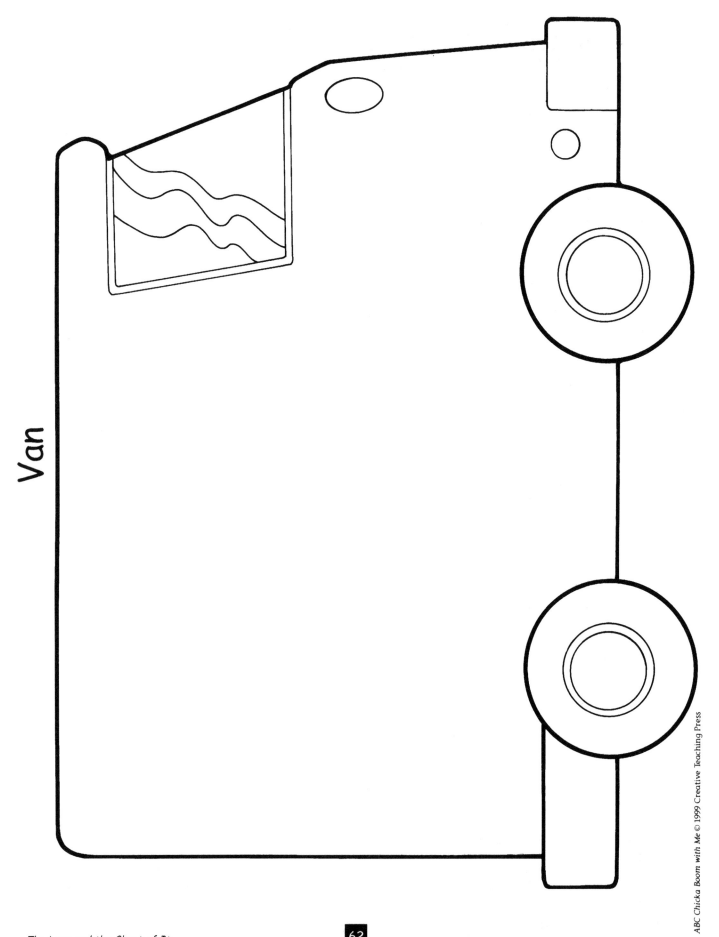

Van

ABC Chicka Boom with Me © 1999 Creative Teaching Press

Braggin' Dragon's Loving Cup Award

The Braggin' Dragon loves the way_____

_____

_____

_____.

_____
Signed

_____
Date

Student Award

Literature Links

A My Name is Alice by Jane Bayer (Dial)

The A to Z Beastly Jamboree by Robert Bender (Lodestar)

The Alphabet Book by P. D. Eastman (Random House)

Ana Banana: 101 Jump-Rope Rhymes by Joanna Cole (Morrow)

Animalia by Graeme Base (Harry N. Abrams)

The Beastly Feast by Bruce Goldstone (Henry Holt & Company)

But Not the Hippopotamus by Sandra Boynton (Simon & Schuster)

Chicka Chicka Boom Boom by Bill Martin Jr. and John Archambault (Simon & Schuster)

Clap Your Hands by Lorinda Bryan Cauley (G. P. Putnam's Sons)

Dr. Seuss' ABC by Dr. Seuss (Random House)

The Dragons Are Singing Tonight by Jack Prelutsky (Greenwillow)

Drummer Hoff by Barbara Emberley (S & S Trade)

Eating the Alphabet: Fruits and Vegetables From A to Z by Lois Ehlert (Harcourt Brace)

Hand Rhymes by Marc Brown (E. P. Dutton)

Hooper Humperdink, Not Him by Theo. LeSieg (Random House)

"I Can't," Said the Ant by Polly Cameron (Scholastic)

I'm a Little Teapot by Iza Trapani (Whispering Coyote)

The Itsy Bitsy Spider by Iza Trapani (Whispering Coyote)

Jamaica Tag-Along by Juanita Hill (Houghton Mifflin)

The Lady With the Alligator Purse by Nadine Bernard Westcott (Little, Brown and Company)

Let's Play: Traditional Games of Childhood by Camilla Gryski (Kids Can)

Miss Bindergarten Gets Ready for Kindergarten by Joseph Slate (Dutton)

Miss Mary Mac and Other Children's Street Rhymes by Joanna Cole and Stephanie Calmenson (Morrow)

Mr. Brown Can Moo, Can You? by Dr. Seuss (Random House)

Polar Bear, Polar Bear by Bill Martin Jr. and Eric Carle (Henry Holt)

Read Aloud Rhymes for the Very Young selected by Jack Prelutsky (Alfred A. Knopf)

Richard Scarry's Splish Splash Sounds by Richard Scarry (Golden)

Shimmy Shimmy Coke-Ca-Pop! by John and Carol Langstaff (Doubleday)

Splash by Ann Jonas (Greenwillow)

Street Rhymes Around the World by Jane Yolen (Wordsong)

There's a Wocket in My Pocket by Dr. Seuss (Random House)

Where Did All the Dragons Go? by Fay Robinson (Bridgewater)

The Z Was Zapped by Chris Van Allsburg (Houghton Mifflin)